A
THEOLOGICO-POLITICAL
TREATISE

PART III
CHAPTERS XI TO XV

A

THEOLOGICO-POLITICAL
TREATISE

PART III
CHAPTERS XI TO XV

By
BENEDICT DE SPINOZA

Also known as
BARUCH SPINOZA

ARC
MANOR
ROCKVILLE, MARYLAND
2008

CONTENTS

CHAPTER XI

An Inquiry Whether the Apostles Wrote Their Epistles
As Apostles and Prophets, or Merely as Teachers; And an
Explanation of What is Meant by an Apostle.

No reader of the New Testament can doubt that the Apostles were prophets; but as a prophet does not always speak by revelation, but only, at rare intervals, as we showed at the end of Chap. I., we may fairly inquire whether the Apostles wrote their Epistles as prophets, by revelation and express mandate, as Moses, Jeremiah, and others did, or whether only as private individuals or teachers, especially as Paul, in Corinthians xiv:6, mentions two sorts of preaching.

If we examine the style of the Epistles, we shall find it totally different from that employed by the prophets.

The prophets are continually asserting that they speak by the command of God: "Thus saith the Lord," "The Lord of hosts saith," "The command of the Lord," &c.; and this was their habit not only in assemblies of the prophets, but also in their epistles containing revelations, as appears from the epistle of Elijah to Jehoram, 2 Chron. xxi:12, which begins, "Thus saith the Lord."

In the Apostolic Epistles we find nothing of the sort. Contrariwise, in I Cor. vii:40 Paul speaks according to his own opinion and in many passages we come across doubtful and perplexed phrase; such as, "We think, therefore," Rom. iii:28; "Now I think," [1] Rom. viii:18, and so on. Besides these, other expressions are met with very different from those used by

---

1   See Endnote 24.

the prophets. For instance, 1 Cor. vii:6, "But I speak this by permission, not by commandment;" "I give my judgment as one that hath obtained mercy of the Lord to be faithful" (1 Cor. vii:25), and so on in many other passages. We must also remark that in the aforesaid chapter the Apostle says that when he states that he has or has not the precept or commandment of God, he does not mean the precept or commandment of God revealed to himself, but only the words uttered by Christ in His Sermon on the Mount. Furthermore, if we examine the manner in which the Apostles give out evangelical doctrine, we shall see that it differs materially from the method adopted by the prophets. The Apostles everywhere reason as if they were arguing rather than prophesying; the prophecies, on the other hand, contain only dogmas and commands. God is therein introduced not as speaking to reason, but as issuing decrees by His absolute fiat. The authority of the prophets does not submit to discussion, for whosoever wishes to find rational ground for his arguments, by that very wish submits them to everyone's private judgment. This Paul, inasmuch as he uses reason, appears to have done, for he says in 1 Cor. x:15, "I speak as to wise men, judge ye what I say." The prophets, as we showed at the end of Chapter I., did not perceive what was revealed by virtue of their natural reason, and though there are certain passages in the Pentateuch which seem to be appeals to induction, they turn out, on nearer examination, to be nothing but peremptory commands. For instance, when Moses says, Deut. xxxi:27, "Behold, while I am yet alive with you, this day ye have been rebellious against the Lord; and how much more after my death," we must by no means conclude that Moses wished to convince the Israelites by reason that they would necessarily fall away from the worship of the Lord after his death; for the argument would have been false, as Scripture itself shows: the Israelites continued faithful during the lives of Joshua and the elders, and afterwards during the time of Samuel, David, and Solomon. Therefore the words of Moses are merely a moral injunction, in which he predicts rhetorically the future backsliding of the people so as to impress it vividly on their imagination. I say that Moses spoke of himself in order to lend likelihood to his prediction, and not as a prophet by revelation, because in verse 21 of the same chapter we are told that God revealed the same thing to Moses in different words, and there was no need to make Moses certain by argument of God's prediction and decree; it was only necessary that it should be vividly impressed on his imagination, and this could not be better accomplished than by imagining the existing contumacy of the people, of which he had had frequent experience, as likely to extend into the future.

All the arguments employed by Moses in the five books are to be understood in a similar manner; they are not drawn from the armoury of reason, but are merely, modes of expression calculated to instil with efficacy, and present vividly to the imagination the commands of God. However, I do not wish absolutely to deny that the prophets ever argued from revelation; I only maintain that the prophets made more legitimate use of argument in proportion as their knowledge approached more nearly to ordinary knowledge, and by this we know that they possessed a knowledge above the ordinary, inasmuch as they proclaimed absolute dogmas, decrees, or judgments. Thus Moses, the chief of the prophets, never used legitimate argument, and, on the other hand, the long deductions and arguments of Paul, such as we find in the Epistle to the Romans, are in nowise written from supernatural revelation.

The modes of expression and discourse adopted by the Apostles in the Epistles, show very clearly that the latter were not written by revelation and Divine command, but merely by the natural powers and judgment of the authors. They consist in brotherly admonitions and courteous expressions such as would never be employed in prophecy, as for instance, Paul's excuse in Romans xv:15, "I have written the more boldly unto you in some sort, my brethren."

We may arrive at the same conclusion from observing that we never read that the Apostles were commanded to write, but only that they went everywhere preaching, and confirmed their words with signs. Their personal presence and signs were absolutely necessary for the conversion and establishment in religion of the Gentiles; as Paul himself expressly states in Rom. i:11, "But I long to see you, that I may impart to you some spiritual gift, to the end that ye may be established."

It may be objected that we might prove in similar fashion that the Apostles did not preach as prophets, for they did not go to particular places, as the prophets did, by the command of God. We read in the Old Testament that Jonah went to Nineveh to preach, and at the same time that he was expressly sent there, and told that he most preach. So also it is related, at great length, of Moses that he went to Egypt as the messenger of God, and was told at the same time what he should say to the children of Israel and to king Pharaoh, and what wonders he should work before them to give credit to his words. Isaiah, Jeremiah, and Ezekiel were expressly commanded to preach to the Israelites. Lastly, the prophets only preached what we are assured by Scripture they had received from God, whereas this is hardly ever said of the Apostles in the New Testament, when they went about to preach. On the contrary, we find passages expressly implying that the Apostles chose the places where they should preach on their own responsibility, for there was a difference amounting to a quarrel between Paul and Barnabas on the subject (Acts xv:37, 38). Often they wished to go to a place, but were prevented, as Paul writes, Rom. i:13, "Oftentimes I purposed to come to you, but was let hitherto;" and in I Cor. xvi:12, "As touching our brother Apollos, I greatly desired him to come unto you with the brethren, but his will was not at all to come at this time: but he will come when he shall have convenient time."

From these expressions and differences of opinion among the Apostles, and also from the fact that Scripture nowhere testifies of them, as of the ancient prophets, that they went by the command of God, one might conclude that they preached as well as wrote in their capacity of teachers, and not as prophets: but the question is easily solved if we observe the difference between the mission of an Apostle and that of an Old Testament prophet. The latter were not called to preach and prophesy to all nations, but to certain specified ones, and therefore an express and peculiar mandate was required for each of them; the Apostles, on the other hand, were called to preach to all men absolutely, and to turn all men to religion. Therefore, whithersoever they went, they were fulfilling Christ's commandment; there was no need to reveal to them beforehand what they should preach, for they were the disciples of Christ to whom their Master Himself said (Matt. x:19, 20): "But, when they deliver you up, take no thought how or what ye shall speak, for it shall be given you in that same hour what ye shall speak." We therefore conclude that the Apostles were only indebted to special revelation in what they orally preached and confirmed by signs (see the beginning of Chap. 11.); that which they taught in speaking or writing without any confirmatory signs and wonders they taught from their natural knowledge. (See I Cor. xiv:6.) We need not be deterred by the fact that all the Epistles begin by citing the imprimatur of the Apostleship, for the Apostles, as I will shortly show, were granted, not only the faculty of prophecy, but also the authority to teach. We may therefore admit that they wrote their Epistles as Apostles, and for this cause every one of them began by citing the Apostolic imprimatur, possibly with a view to the attention of the reader by asserting that they were the persons who had made such mark among the faithful by their preaching, and had shown bv many marvelous works that they were teaching true religion and the way of salvation. I observe that what is said in the Epistles with regard to the Apostolic vocation and the Holy Spirit of God which inspired them, has reference to their former preaching, except in those passages where the expressions of the Spirit of God and the Holy Spirit are used to signify a mind pure, upright, and devoted to God. For instance, in 1 Cor. vii:40, Paul says: But she is happier if she so abide, after my judgment, and I think also that I have the Spirit of God." By the Spirit of God the Apostle here refers to his mind, as we may see from the context: his meaning is as follows: "I account blessed a widow who does not wish to marry a second husband; such is my opinion, for I have settled to live unmarried, and I think that I am blessed." There are other similar passages which I need not now quote.

As we have seen that the Apostles wrote their Epistles solely by the light of natural reason, we must inquire how they were enabled to teach by natural knowledge matters outside its scope. However, if we bear in mind what we said in Chap. vii. of this treatise our difficulty will vanish: for although the contents of the Bible entirely surpass our understanding, we may safely discourse of them, provided we assume nothing not told us in Scripture: by the same method the Apostles, from what they saw and heard, and from what was revealed to them, were enabled to form and elicit many conclusions which they would have been able to teach to men had it been permissible.

Further, although religion, as preached by the Apostles, does not come within the sphere of reason, in so far as it consists in the narration of the life of Christ, yet its essence, which is chiefly moral, like the whole of Christ's doctrine, can readily, be apprehended by the natural faculties of all.

Lastly, the Apostles had no lack of supernatural illumination for the purpose of adapting the religion they had attested by signs to the understanding of everyone so that it might be readily received; nor for exhortations on the subject: in fact, the object of the Epistles is to teach and exhort men to lead that manner of life which each of the Apostles judged best for confirming them in religion. We may here repeat our former remark, that the Apostles had received not only the faculty of preaching the history, of Christ as prophets, and confirming it with signs, but also authority for teaching and exhorting according as each thought best. Paul (2 Tim. i:11), "Whereunto I am appointed a preacher, and an apostle, and a teacher of the Gentiles;" and again (I Tim. ii:7), "Whereunto I am ordained a preacher and an apostle (I speak the truth in Christ and lie not), a teacher of the Gentiles in faith and verity." These passages, I say, show clearly the stamp both of the apostleship and the teachership: the authority for admonishing whomsoever and wheresoever he pleased is asserted by Paul in the Epistle to Philemon, v:8: "Wherefore, though I might be much bold in Christ to enjoin thee that which is convenient, yet," &c., where we may remark that if Paul had received from God as a prophet what he wished to enjoin Philemon, and had been bound to speak in his prophetic capacity, he would not have been able to change the command of God into entreaties. We must therefore understand him to refer to the permission to admonish which he had received as a teacher, and not as a prophet. We have not yet made it quite clear that the Apostles might each choose his own way of teaching, but only that by virtue of their Apostleship they were teachers as well as prophets; however, if we call reason to our aid we shall clearly see that an authority to teach implies authority to choose the method. It will nevertheless be, perhaps, more satisfactory to draw all our proofs from Scripture; we are there plainly told that each Apostle chose his particular method (Rom. xv: 20): "Yea, so have I strived to preach the gospel, not where Christ was named, lest I should build upon another man's foundation." If all the Apostles had adopted the same method of teaching, and had all built up the Christian religion on the same foundation, Paul would have had no reason to call the work of a fellow-Apostle "another man's foundation," inasmuch as it would have been identical with his own: his calling it another man's proved that each Apostle built up his religious instruction on different foundations, thus resembling other teachers who have each their own method, and prefer instructing quite ignorant people who have never learnt under another master, whether the subject be science, languages, or even the indisputable truths of mathematics. Furthermore, if we go through the Epistles at all attentively, we shall see that the Apostles, while agreeing about religion itself, are at variance as to the foundations it rests on. Paul, in order to strengthen men's religion, and show them that salvation depends solely on the grace of God, teaches that no one can boast of works, but only of faith, and that no one can be justified by works (Rom. iii:27,28); in fact, he preaches the complete doctrine of predestination. James, on the other hand, states that man is justified by works, and not by faith only (see his Epistle, ii:24), and omitting all the disputations of Paul, confines religion to a very few elements.

Lastly, it is indisputable that from these different ground; for religion selected by the Apostles, many quarrels and schisms distracted the Church, even in the earliest times, and doubt-less they will continue so to distract it for ever, or at least till religion is separated from philosophical speculations, and re-duced to the few simple doctrines taught by Christ to His dis-ciples; such a task was impossible for the Apostles, because the Gospel was then unknown to mankind, and lest its nov-elty should offend men's ears it had to be adapted to the dis-position of contemporaries (2 Cor. ix:19, 20), and built up on the groundwork most familiar and accepted at the time. Thus none of the Apostles philosophized more than did Paul, who was called to preach to the Gentiles; other Apostles preach-ing to the Jews, who despised philosophy, similarly, adapted themselves to the temper of their hearers (see Gal. ii. 11), and preached a religion free from all philosophical speculations. How blest would our age be if it could witness a religion freed also from all the trammels of superstition!

CHAPTER XII

Of the True Original of the Divine Law, And Wherefore Scripture is Called Sacred, and the Word of God. How That, in So Far as it Contains the Word of God, It Has Come Down to Us Uncorrupted.

THOSE who look upon the Bible as a message sent down by God from Heaven to men, will doubtless cry out that I have committed the sin against the Holy Ghost because I have asserted that the Word of God is faulty, mutilated, tampered with, and inconsistent; that we possess it only in fragments, and that the original of the covenant which God made with the Jews has been lost. However, I have no doubt that a little reflection will cause them to desist from their uproar: for not only reason but the expressed opinions of prophets and apostles openly proclaim that God's eternal Word and covenant, no less than true religion, is Divinely inscribed in human hearts, that is, in the human mind, and that this is the true original of God's covenant, stamped with His own seal, namely, the idea of Himself, as it were, with the image of His Godhood.

Religion was imparted to the early Hebrews as a law written down, because they were at that time in the condition of children, but afterwards Moses (Deut. xxx:6) and Jeremiah (xxxi:33) predicted a time coming when the Lord should write His law in their hearts. Thus only the Jews, and amongst them chiefly the Sadducees, struggled for the law written on tablets; least of all need those who bear it inscribed on their hearts join in the contest. Those, therefore, who reflect, will find nothing in what I have written repugnant either to the Word of God or to true religion and faith, or calculated to weaken either one or the other: contrariwise, they will see that I have strengthened religion, as I showed at the end of Chapter x.; indeed, had it not been so, I should certainly have decided to hold my peace, nay, I would even have asserted as a way out of all difficulties that the Bible contains the most profound hidden mysteries; however, as this doctrine has given rise to gross superstition and other pernicious results spoken of at the beginning of Chapter v., I have thought such a course unnecessary, especially as religion stands in no need of superstitious adornments, but is, on the contrary, deprived by such trappings of some of her splendour.

Still, it will be said, though the law of God is written in the heart, the Bible is none the less the Word of God, and it is no more lawful to say of Scripture than of God's Word that it is mutilated and corrupted. I fear that such objectors are too anxious to be pious, and that they are in danger of turning religion into superstition, and worshipping paper and ink in place of God's Word.

I am certified of thus much: I have said nothing unworthy of Scripture or God's Word, and I have made no assertions which I could not prove by most plain argument to be true. I can, therefore, rest assured that I have advanced nothing which is impious or even savours of impiety.

from what I have said, assume a licence to sin, and without any reason, at I confess that some profane men, to whom religion is a burden, may, the simple dictates of their lusts conclude that Scripture is everywhere faulty and falsified, and that therefore its authority is null; but such men are beyond the reach of help, for nothing, as the pro verb has it, can be said so rightly that it cannot be twisted into wrong. Those who wish to give rein to their lusts are at no loss for an excuse, nor were those men of old who possessed the original Scriptures, the ark of the covenant, nay, the prophets and apostles in person among them, any better than the people of to-day. Human nature, Jew as well as Gentile, has always been the same, and in every age virtue has been exceedingly rare.

Nevertheless, to remove every scruple, I will here show in what sense the Bible or any inanimate thing should be called sacred and Divine; also wherein the law of God consists, and how it cannot be contained in a certain number of books; and, lastly, I will show that Scripture, in so far as it teaches what is necessary for obedience and salvation, cannot have been corrupted. From these considerations everyone will be able to judge that I have neither said anything against the Word of God nor given any foothold to impiety.

A thing is called sacred and Divine when it is designed for promoting piety, and continues sacred so long as it is religiously used: if the users cease to be pious, the thing ceases to be sacred: if it be turned to base uses, that which was formerly sacred becomes unclean and profane. For instance, a certain spot was named by the patriarch Jacob the house of God, because he worshipped God there revealed to him: by the prophets the same spot was called the house of iniquity (see Amos v:5, and Hosea x:5), because the Israelites were wont, at the instigation of Jeroboam, to sacrifice there to idols. Another example puts the matter in the plainest light. Words gain their meaning solely from their usage, and if they are arranged according to their accepted signification so as to move those who read them to devotion, they will become sacred, and the book so written will be sacred also. But if their usage afterwards dies out so that the words have no meaning, or the book becomes utterly neglected, whether from unworthy motives, or because it is no longer needed, then the words and the book will lose both their use and their sanctity: lastly, if these same words be otherwise arranged, or if their customary meaning becomes perverted into its opposite, then both the words and the book containing them become, instead of sacred, impure and profane.

From this it follows that nothing is in itself absolutely sacred, or profane, and unclean, apart from the mind, but only relatively thereto. Thus much is clear from many passages in the Bible. Jeremiah (to select one case out of many) says (chap. vii:4), that the Jews of his time were wrong in calling Solomon's Temple, the Temple of God, for, as he goes on to say in the same chapter, God's name would only be given to the Temple so long as it was frequented by men who worshipped Him, and defended justice, but that, if it became the resort of murderers, thieves, idolaters, and other wicked persons, it would be turned into a den of malefactors.

Scripture, curiously enough, nowhere tells us what became of the Ark of the Covenant, though there is no doubt that it was destroyed, or burnt together with the Temple; yet there was nothing which the Hebrews considered more sacred, or held in greater reverence. Thus Scripture is sacred, and its words Divine so long as it stirs mankind to devotion towards God: but if it be utterly neglected, as it formerly was by the Jews, it becomes nothing but paper and ink, and is left to be desecrated or corrupted: still, though Scripture be thus corrupted or destroyed, we must not say that the Word of God has suffered in like manner, else we shall be like the Jews, who said that the Temple which would then be the Temple of God had perished in the flames. Jeremiah tells us this in respect to the law, for he thus chides the ungodly of his time, "Wherefore, say you we are masters, and the law of the Lord is with us? Surely it has been given in vain, it is in vain that the pen of the scribes " (has been made)—that is, you say falsely that the Scripture is in your power, and that you possess the law of God; for ye have made it of none effect.

So also, when Moses broke the first tables of the law, he did not by any means cast the Word of God from his hands in anger and shatter it—such an action would be inconceivable, either of Moses or of God's Word—he only broke the tables of stone, which, though they had before been holy from containing the covenant wherewith the Jews had bound themselves in obedience to God, had entirely lost their sanctity when the covenant had been violated by the worship of the calf, and were, therefore, as liable to perish as the ark of the covenant. It is thus scarcely to be wondered at, that the original documents of Moses are no longer extant, nor that the books we possess met with the fate we have described, when we consider that the true original of the Divine covenant, the most sacred object of all, has totally perished.

Let them cease, therefore, who accuse us of impiety, inasmuch as we have said nothing against the Word of God, neither have we corrupted it, but let them keep their anger, if they would wreak it justly, for the ancients whose malice desecrated the Ark, the Temple, and the Law of God, and all that was held sacred, subjecting them to corruption. Furthermore, if, according to the saying of the Apostle in 2 Cor. iii:3, they possessed "the Epistle of Christ, written not with ink, but with the Spirit of the living God, not in tables of stone, but in the fleshy tables of the heart," let them cease to worship the letter, and be so anxious concerning it.

I think I have now sufficiently shown in what respect Scripture should be accounted sacred and Divine; we may now see what should rightly be understood by the expression, the Word of the Lord; debar (the Hebrew original) signifies word, speech, command, and thing. The causes for which a thing is in Hebrew said to be of God, or is referred to Him, have been already detailed in Chap. I., and we can therefrom easily gather what meaning Scripture attaches to the phrases, the word, the speech, the command, or the thing of God. I need not, therefore, repeat what I there said, nor what was shown under the third head in the chapter on miracles. It is enough to mention the repetition for the better understanding of what I am about to say—viz., that the Word of the Lord when it has reference to anyone but God Himself, signifies that Divine law treated of in Chap. iv.; in other words, religion, universal and catholic to the whole human race, as Isaiah describes it (chap. i:10), teaching that the true way of life consists, not in ceremonies, but in charity, and a true heart, and calling it indifferently God's Law and God's Word.

The expression is also used metaphorically for the order of nature and destiny (which, indeed, actually depend and follow from the eternal mandate of the Divine nature), and especially for such parts of such order as were foreseen by the prophets, for the prophets did not perceive future events as the result of natural causes, but as the fiats and decrees of God. Lastly, it is employed for the command of any prophet, in so far as he had perceived it by his peculiar faculty or prophetic gift, and not by the natural light of reason; this use springs chiefly from the usual prophetic conception of God as a legislator, which we remarked in Chap. IV. There are, then, three causes for the Bible's being called the Word of God: because it teaches true religion, of which God is the eternal Founder; because it narrates predictions of future events as though they were decrees of God; because its actual authors generally perceived things not by their ordinary natural faculties, but by a power peculiar to themselves, and introduced these things perceived, as told them by God.

Although Scripture contains much that is merely historical and can be perceived by natural reason, yet its name is acquired from its chief subject matter.

We can thus easily see how God can be said to be the Author of the Bible: it is because of the true religion therein contained, and not because He wished to communicate to men a certain number of books. We can also learn from hence the reason for the division into Old and New Testament. It was made because the prophets who preached religion before Christ, preached it as a national law in virtue of the covenant entered into under Moses; while the Apostles who came after Christ, preached it to all men as a universal religion solely in virtue of Christ's Passion: the cause for the division is not that the two parts are different in doctrine, nor that they were written as originals of the covenant, nor, lastly, that the catholic religion (which is in entire harmony with our nature) was new except in relation to those who had not known it: " it was in the world," as John the Evangelist says, " and the world knew it not."

Thus, even if we had fewer books of the Old and New Testament than we have, we should still not be deprived of the Word of God (which, as we have said, is identical with true religion), even as we do not now hold ourselves to be deprived of it, though we lack many cardinal writings such as the Book of the Law, which was religiously guarded in the Temple as the original of the Covenant, also the Book of Wars, the Book of Chronicles, and many others, from whence the extant Old

Testament was taken and compiled. The above conclusion may be supported by many reasons.

I. Because the books of both Testaments were not written by express command at one place for all ages, but are a fortuitous collection of the works of men, writing each as his period and disposition dictated. So much is clearly shown by the call of the prophets who were bade to admonish the ungodly of their time, and also by the Apostolic Epistles.

II. Because it is one thing to understand the meaning of Scripture and the prophets, and quite another thing to understand the meaning of God, or the actual truth. This follows from what we said in Chap. II. We showed, in Chap. VI., that it applied to historic narratives, and to miracles: but it by no means applies to questions concerning true religion and virtue.

III. Because the books of the Old Testament were selected from many, and were collected and sanctioned by a council of the Pharisees, as we showed in Chap. X. The books of the New Testament were also chosen from many by councils which rejected as spurious other books held sacred by many. But these councils, both Pharisee and Christian, were not composed of prophets, but only of learned men and teachers. Still, we must grant that they were guided in their choice by a regard for the Word of God ; and they must, therefore, have known what the law of God was.

IV. Because the Apostles wrote not as prophets, but as teachers (see last Chapter), and chose whatever method they thought best adapted for those whom they addressed: and consequently, there are many things in the Epistles (as we showed at the end of the last Chapter) which are not necessary to salvation.

V. Lastly, because there are four Evangelists in the New Testament, and it is scarcely credible that God can have designed to narrate the life of Christ four times over, and to communicate it thus to mankind. For though there are some details related in one Gospel which are not in another, and one often helps us to understand another, we cannot thence conclude that all that is set down is of vital importance to us, and that God chose the four Evangelists in order that the life of Christ might be better understood; for each one preached his Gospel in a separate locality, each wrote it down as he preached it, in simple language, in order that the history of Christ might be clearly told, not with any view of explaining his fellow-Evangelists.

If there are some passages which can be better, and more easily understood by comparing the various versions, they are the result of chance, and are not numerous: their continuance in obscurity would have impaired neither the clearness of the narrative nor the blessedness of mankind.

We have now shown that Scripture can only be called the Word of God in so far as it affects religion, or the Divine law; we must now point out that, in respect to these questions, it is neither faulty, tampered with, nor corrupt. By faulty, tampered with, and corrupt, I here mean written so incorrectly, that the meaning cannot be arrived at by a study of the language, nor from the authority of Scripture. I will not go to such lengths as to say that the Bible, in so far as it contains the Divine law, has always preserved the same vowel-points, the same letters, or the same words (I leave this to be proved by, the Massoretes and other worshippers of the letter), I only, maintain that the meaning by, which alone an utterance is entitled to be called Divine, has come down to us uncorrupted, even though the original wording may have been more often changed than we suppose. Such alterations, as I have said above, detract nothing from the Divinity of the Bible, for the Bible would have been no less Divine had it been written in different words or a different language. That the Divine law has in this sense come down to us uncorrupted, is an assertion which admits of no dispute. For from the Bible itself we learn, without the smallest difficulty or ambiguity,, that its cardinal precept is: To love God above all things, and one's neighbour as one's self. This cannot be a spurious passage, nor due to a hasty and mistaken scribe, for if the Bible had ever put forth a different doctrine it would have had to change the whole of its teaching, for this is the corner-stone of religion, without which the whole fabric would fall headlong to the ground. The Bible would not be the work we have been examining, but something quite different.

We remain, then, unshaken in our belief that this has always been the doctrine of Scripture, and, consequently, that no error sufficient to vitiate it can have crept in without being instantly, observed by all; nor can anyone have succeeded in tampering with it and escaped the discovery of his malice.

As this corner-stone is intact, we must perforce admit the same of whatever other passages are indisputably dependent on it, and are also fundamental, as, for instance, that a God exists, that He foresees all things, that He is Almighty, that by His decree the good prosper and the wicked come to naught, and, finally, that our salvation depends solely on His grace.

These are doctrines which Scripture plainly teaches throughout, and which it is bound to teach, else all the rest would be empty and baseless; nor can we be less positive about other moral doctrines, which plainly are built upon this universal foundation—for instance, to uphold justice, to aid the weak, to do no murder, to covet no man's goods, &c. Precepts, I repeat, such as these, human malice and the lapse of ages are alike powerless to destroy, for if any part of them perished, its loss would immediately be supplied from the fundamental principle, especially the doctrine of charity, which is everywhere in both Testaments extolled above all others. Moreover, though it be true that there is no conceivable crime so heinous that it has never been committed, still there is no one who would attempt in excuse for his crimes to destroy, the law, or introduce an impious doctrine in the place of what is eternal and salutary; men's nature is so constituted that everyone (be he king or subject) who has committed a base action, tries to deck out his conduct with spurious excuses, till he seems to have done nothing but what is just and right.

We may conclude, therefore, that the whole Divine law, as taught by Scripture, has come down to us uncorrupted. Besides this there are certain facts which we may be sure have been transmitted in good faith. For instance, the main facts of Hebrew history, which were perfectly well known to everyone. The Jewish people were accustomed in former times to chant the ancient history of their nation in psalms. The main facts, also, of Christ's life and passion were immediately spread abroad through the whole Roman empire. It is therefore scarcely credible, unless nearly everybody, consented thereto, which we cannot suppose, that successive generations have handed down the broad outline of the Gospel narrative otherwise than as they received it.

Whatsoever, therefore, is spurious or faulty can only have reference to details—some circumstances in one or the other history or prophecy designed to stir the people to greater devotion; or in some miracle, with a view of confounding philosophers; or, lastly, in speculative matters after they had become mixed up with religion, so that some individual might prop up his own inventions with a pretext of Divine authority. But such matters have little to do with salvation, whether they be corrupted little or much, as I will show in detail in the next chapter, though I think the question sufficiently plain from what I have said already, especially in Chapter II.

CHAPTER XIII

It is Shown That Scripture Teaches Only Very Simple Doctrines, Such as Suffice for Right Conduct

IN the second chapter of this treatise we pointed out that the prophets were gifted with extraordinary powers of imagination, but not of understanding; also that God only revealed to them such things as are very simple—not philosophic mysteries,—and that He adapted His communications to their previous opinions. We further showed in Chap. v. that Scripture only transmits and teaches truths which can readily be comprehended by all; not deducing and concatenating its conclusions from definitions and axioms, but narrating quite simply, and confirming its statements, with a view to inspiring belief, by an appeal to experience as exemplified in miracles and history, and setting forth its truths in the style and phraseology which would most appeal to the popular mind (cf. Chap. vi., third division).

Lastly, we demonstrated in Chap. viii. that the difficulty of understanding Scripture lies in the language only, and not in the abstruseness of the argument.

To these considerations we may add that the Prophets did not preach only to the learned, but to all Jews, without exception, while the Apostles were wont to teach the gospel doctrine in churches where there were public meetings; whence it follows that Scriptural doctrine contains no lofty speculations nor philosophic reasoning, but only very simple matters, such as could be understood by the slowest intelligence.

I am consequently lost in wonder at the ingenuity of those whom I have already mentioned, who detect in the Bible mysteries so profound that they cannot be explained in human language, and who have introduced so many philosophic speculations into religion that the Church seems like an academy, and religion like a science, or rather a dispute.

It is not to be wondered at that men, who boast of possessing supernatural intelligence, should be unwilling to yield the palm of knowledge to philosophers who have only their ordinary, faculties; still I should be surprised if I found them teaching any new speculative doctrine, which was not a commonplace to those Gentile philosophers whom, in spite of all, they stigmatize as blind; for, if one inquires what these mysteries lurking in Scripture may be, one is confronted with nothing but the reflections of Plato or Aristotle, or the like, which it would often be easier for an ignorant man to dream than for the most accomplished scholar to wrest out of the Bible.

However, I do not wish to affirm absolutely that Scripture contains no doctrines in the sphere of philosophy, for in the last chapter I pointed out some of the kind, as fundamental principles; but I go so far as to say that such doctrines are very few and very simple. Their precise nature and definition I will now set forth. The task will be easy, for we know that Scripture does not aim at imparting scientific knowledge, and, therefore, it demands from men nothing but obedience, and censures obstinacy, but not ignorance.

Furthermore, as obedience to God consists solely in love to our neighbour—for whosoever loveth his neighbour, as a means of obeying God, hath, as St. Paul says (Rom. xiii:8), fulfilled the law,—it follows that no knowledge is commended in the Bible save that which is necessary for enabling all men to obey God in the manner stated, and without which they would become rebellious, or without the discipline of obedience.

Other speculative questions, which have no direct bearing on this object, or are concerned with the knowledge of natural events, do not affect Scripture, and should be entirely separated from religion.

Now, though everyone, as we have said, is now quite able to see this truth for himself, I should nevertheless wish, considering that the whole of Religion depends thereon, to explain the entire question more accurately and clearly. To this end I must first prove that the intellectual or accurate knowledge of God is not a gift, bestowed upon all good men like obedience; and, further, that the knowledge of God, required by Him through His prophets from everyone without exception, as needful to be known, is simply a knowledge of His Divine justice and charity. Both these points are easily proved from Scripture. The first plainly follows from Exodus vi:2, where God, in order to show the singular grace bestowed upon Moses, says to him: "And I appeared unto Abraham, unto Isaac, and unto Jacob by the name of El Sadai (A. V. God Almighty); but by my name Jehovah was I not known to them"—for the better understanding of which passage I may remark that El Sadai, in Hebrew, signifies the God who suffices, in that He gives to every man that which suffices for him; and, although Sadai is often used by itself, to signify God, we cannot doubt that the word El (God, {power, might}) is everywhere understood. Furthermore, we must note that Jehovah is the only word found in Scripture with the meaning of the absolute essence of God, without reference to created things. The Jews maintain, for this reason, that this is, strictly speaking, the only name of God; that the rest of the words used are merely titles; and, in truth, the other names of God, whether they be substantives or adjectives, are merely attributive, and belong to Him, in so far as He is conceived of in relation to created things, or manifested through them. Thus El, or Eloah, signifies powerful, as is well known, and only applies to God in respect to His supremacy, as when we call Paul an apostle; the faculties of his power are set forth in an accompanying adjective, as El, great, awful, just, merciful, &c., or else all are understood at once by the use of El in the plural number, with a singular signification, an expression frequently adopted in Scripture.

Now, as God tells Moses that He was not known to the patriarchs by the name of Jehovah, it follows that they were not cognizant of any attribute of God which expresses His absolute essence, but only of His deeds and promises that is, of His power, as manifested in visible things. God does not thus speak to Moses in order to accuse the patriarchs of infidelity, but, on the contrary, as a means of extolling their belief and faith, inasmuch as, though they possessed no extraordinary knowledge of God (such as Moses had), they yet accepted His promises as fixed and certain; whereas Moses, though his thoughts about God were more exalted, nevertheless doubted about the Divine promises, and complained to God that, instead of the promised deliverance, the prospects of the Israelites had darkened.

As the patriarchs did not know the distinctive name of God, and as God mentions the fact to Moses, in praise of their faith and single-heartedness, and in contrast to the extraordinary grace granted to Moses, it follows, as we stated at first, that men are not bound by, decree to have knowledge of the attributes of God, such knowledge being only granted to a few of the faithful: it is hardly worth while to quote further examples from Scripture, for everyone must recognize that knowledge of God is not equal among all good men. Moreover, a man cannot be ordered to be wise any more than he can be ordered to live and exist. Men, women, and children are all alike able to obey by, commandment, but not to be wise. If any tell us that it is not necessary to understand the Divine attributes, but that we must believe them simply, without proof, he is plainly, trifling. For what is invisible and can only, be perceived by the mind, cannot be apprehended by any, other means than proofs; if these are absent the object remains ungrasped; the repetition of what has been heard on such subjects no more indicates or attains to their meaning than the words of a parrot or a puppet speaking without sense or signification.

Before I proceed I ought to explain how it comes that we are often told in Genesis that the patriarchs preached in the name of Jehovah, this being in plain contradiction to the text above quoted. A reference to what was said in Chap. VIII. will readily explain the difficulty. It was there shown that the writer of the Pentateuch did not always speak of things and places by the names they bore in the times of which he was writing, but by the names best known to his contemporaries. God is thus said in the Pentateuch to have been preached by the patriarchs under the name of Jehovah, not because such was the name by which the patriarchs knew Him, but because this name was the one most reverenced by the Jews. This point, I say, must necessarily be noticed, for in Exodus it is expressly stated that God was not known to the patriarchs by this name; and in chap. iii:13, it is said that Moses desired to know the name of God. Now, if this name had been already known it would have been known to Moses. We must therefore draw the conclusion indicated, namely, that the faithful patriarchs did not know this name of God, and that the knowledge of God is bestowed and not commanded by the Deity.

It is now time to pass on to our second point, and show that God through His prophets required from men no other knowledge of Himself than is contained in a knowledge of His justice and charity—that is, of attributes which a certain manner of life will enable men to imitate. Jeremiah states this in so many words (xxii:15, 16): "Did not thy father eat, and drink, and do judgment and justice? and then it was well with him. He judged the cause of the poor and needy; then it was well with him: was not this to know Me ? saith the Lord." The words in chap. ix:24 of the same book are equally, clear. "But let him that glorieth glory in this, that he understandeth and knoweth Me, that I am the Lord which exercise loving-kindness, judgment, and righteousness in the earth; for in these things I delight, saith the Lord." The same doctrine maybe gathered from Exod. xxxiv:6, where God revealed to Moses only, those of His attributes which display the Divine justice and charity. Lastly, we may call attention to a passage in John which we shall discuss at more length hereafter; the Apostle explains the nature of God (inasmuch as no one has beheld Him) through charity only, and concludes that he who possesses charity possesses, and in very, truth knows God.

We have thus seen that Moses, Jeremiah, and John sum up in a very short compass the knowledge of God needful for all, and that they state it to consist in exactly what we said, namely, that God is supremely just, and supremely merciful—in other words, the one perfect pattern of the true life. We may add that Scripture nowhere gives an express definition of God, and does not point out any other of His attributes which should be apprehended save these, nor does it in set terms praise any others. Wherefore we may draw the general conclusion that an intellectual knowledge of God, which takes cognizance of His nature in so far as it actually is, and which cannot by any manner of living be imitated by mankind or followed as an example, has no bearing whatever on true rules of conduct, on faith, or on revealed religion; consequently that men may be in complete error on the subject without incurring the charge of sinfulness. We need now no longer wonder that God adapted Himself to the existing opinions and imaginations of the prophets, or that the faithful held different ideas of God, as we showed in Chap. II.; or, again, that the sacred books speak very inaccurately of God, attributing to Him hands, feet, eyes, ears, a mind, and motion from one place to another; or that they ascribe to Him emotions, such as jealousy, mercy, &c., or, lastly, that they describe Him as a Judge in heaven sitting on a royal throne with Christ on His right hand. Such expressions are adapted to the understanding of the multitude, it being the object of the Bible to make men not learned but obedient.

In spite of this the general run of theologians, when they come upon any of these phrases which they cannot rationally harmonize with the Divine nature, maintain that they should be interpreted metaphorically, passages they cannot understand they say should be interpreted literally. But if every expression of this kind in the Bible is necessarily to be interpreted and understood metaphorically, Scripture must have been written, not for the people and the unlearned masses, but chiefly for accomplished experts and philosophers.

If it were indeed a sin to hold piously and simply the ideas about God we have just quoted, the prophets ought to have been strictly on their guard against the use of such expressions, seeing the weak-mindedness of the people, and ought, on the other hand, to have set forth first of all, duly and clearly, those attributes of God which are needful to be understood.

This they have nowhere done; we cannot, therefore, think that opinions taken in themselves without respect to actions are either pious or impious, but must maintain that a man is pious or impious in his beliefs only in so far as he is thereby incited to obedience, or derives from them license to sin and rebel. If a man, by believing what is true, becomes rebellious, his creed is impious; if by believing what is false he becomes obedient, his creed is pious; for the true knowledge of God comes not by commandment, but by Divine gift. God has required nothing from man but a knowledge of His Divine justice and charity, and that not as necessary to scientific accuracy, but to obedience.

CHAPTER XIV

*Definitions of Faith, the Faith, and the Foundations
Of Faith, Which is Once for All Separated from Philosophy*

FOR a true knowledge of faith it is above all things necessary to understand that the Bible was adapted to the intelligence, not only of the prophets, but also of the diverse and
fickle Jewish multitude. This will be recognized by all who
give any thought to the subject, for they will see that a person who accepted promiscuously everything in Scripture as
being the universal and absolute teaching of God, without
accurately defining what was adapted to the popular intelligence, would find it impossible to escape confounding the
opinions of the masses with the Divine doctrines, praising
the judgments and comments of man as the teaching of God,
and making a wrong use of Scriptural authority. Who, I say,
does not perceive that this is the chief reason why so many
sectaries teach contradictory opinions as Divine documents,
and support their contentions with numerous Scriptural
texts, till it has passed in Belgium into a proverb, geen ketter
sonder letter—no heretic without a text? The sacred books
were not written by one man, nor for the people of a single
period, but by many authors of different temperaments, at
times extending from first to last over nearly two thousand
years, and perhaps much longer. We will not, however, accuse
the sectaries of impiety because they have adapted the words
of Scripture to their own opinions; it is thus that these words
were adapted to the understanding of the masses originally,
and everyone is at liberty so to treat them if he sees that he
can thus obey God in matters relating to justice and charity

with a more full consent: but we do accuse those who will not grant this freedom to their fellows, but who persecute all who differ from them, as God's enemies, however honourable and virtuous be their lives; while, on the other hand, they cherish those who agree with them, however foolish they may be, as God's elect. Such conduct is as wicked and dangerous to the state as any that can be conceived.

In order, therefore, to establish the limits to which individual freedom should extend, and to decide what persons, in spite of the diversity of their opinions, are to be looked upon as the faithful, we must define faith and its essentials. This task I hope to accomplish in the present chapter, and also to separate faith from philosophy, which is the chief aim of the whole treatise.

In order to proceed duly to the demonstration let us recapitulate the chief aim and object of Scripture; this will indicate a standard by which we may define faith.

We have said in a former chapter that the aim and object of Scripture is only to teach obedience. Thus much, I think, no one can question. Who does not see that both Testaments are nothing else but schools for this object, and have neither of them any aim beyond inspiring mankind with a voluntary obedience? For (not to repeat what I said in the last chapter) I will remark that Moses did not seek to convince the Jews by reason, but bound them by a covenant, by oaths, and by conferring benefits; further, he threatened the people with punishment if they should infringe the law, and promised rewards if they should obey it. All these are not means for teaching knowledge, but for inspiring obedience. The doctrine of the Gospels enjoins nothing but simple faith, namely, to believe in God and to honour Him, which is the same thing as to obey him. There is no occasion for me to throw further light on a question so plain by citing Scriptural texts commending obedience, such as may be found in great numbers in both Testaments. Moreover, the Bible teaches very clearly in a great many passages what everyone ought to do in order to obey God; the whole duty is summed up in love to one's neighbour. It cannot, therefore, be denied that he who by God's command loves his neighbour as himself is truly obedient and blessed according to the law, whereas he who hates his neighbour or neglects him is rebellious and obstinate.

Lastly, it is plain to everyone that the Bible was not written and disseminated only, for the learned, but for men of every age and race; wherefore we may, rest assured that we are not bound by Scriptural command to believe anything beyond what is absolutely necessary, for fulfilling its main precept.

This precept, then, is the only standard of the whole Catholic faith, and by it alone all the dogmas needful to be believed should be determined. So much being abundantly manifest, as is also the fact that all other doctrines of the faith can be legitimately deduced therefrom by reason alone, I leave it to every man to decide for himself how it comes to pass that so many divisions have arisen in the Church: can it be from any other cause than those suggested at the beginning of Chap. VIII.? It is these same causes which compel me to explain the method of determining the dogmas of the faith from the foundation we have discovered, for if I neglected to do so, and put the question on a regular basis, I might justly be said to have promised too lavishly, for that anyone might, by my showing, introduce any doctrine he liked into religion, under the pretext that it was a necessary means to obedience: especially would this be the case in questions respecting the Divine attributes.

In order, therefore, to set forth the whole matter methodically, I will begin with a definition of faith, which on the principle above given, should be as follows:-

Faith consists in a knowledge of God, without which obedience to Him would be impossible, and which the mere fact of obedience to Him implies. This definition is so clear, and follows so plainly from what we have already proved, that it needs no explanation. The consequences involved therein I will now briefly show.

I. Faith is not salutary in itself, but only in respect to the obedience it implies, or as James puts it in his Epistle, ii:17, "Faith without works is dead" (see the whole of the chapter quoted).

II. He who is truly obedient necessarily possesses true and saving faith; for if obedience be granted, faith must be granted also, as the same Apostle expressly says in these words (ii:18), "Show me thy faith without thy works, and I will show thee my faith by my works." So also John, I Ep. iv:7: "Everyone that loveth is born of God, and knoweth God: he that loveth not, knoweth not God; for God is love." From these texts, I repeat, it follows that we can only judge a man faithful or unfaithful by his works. If his works be good, he is faithful, however much his doctrines may differ from those of the rest of the faithful: if his works be evil, though he may verbally conform, he is unfaithful. For obedience implies faith, and faith without works is dead.

John, in the 13th verse of the chapter above quoted, expressly teaches the same doctrine: "Hereby," he says, "know we that we dwell in Him and He in us, because He hath given us of His Spirit," i.e. love. He had said before that God is love, and therefore he concludes (on his own received principles), that whoso possesses love possesses truly the Spirit of God. As no one has beheld God he infers that no one has knowledge or consciousness of God, except from love towards his neighbour, and also that no one can have knowledge of any of God's attributes, except this of love, in so far as we participate therein.

If these arguments are not conclusive, they, at any rate, show the Apostle's meaning, but the words in chap. ii:3, 4, of the same Epistle are much clearer, for they state in so many words our precise contention: "And hereby we do know that we know Him, if we keep His commandments. He that saith, I know Him, and keepeth not His commandments, is a liar, and the truth is not in him."

From all this, I repeat, it follows that they are the true enemies of Christ who persecute honourable and justice-loving men because they differ from them, and do not uphold the same religious dogmas as themselves: for whosoever loves justice and charity we know, by that very fact, to be faithful: whosoever persecutes the faithful, is an enemy to Christ.

Lastly, it follows that faith does not demand that dogmas should be true as that they should be pious—that is, such as will stir up the heart to obey; though there be many such which contain not a shadow of truth, so long as they be held in good faith, otherwise their adherents are disobedient, for how can anyone, desirous of loving justice and obeying God, adore as Divine what he knows to be alien from the Divine nature? However, men may err from simplicity of mind, and Scripture, as we have seen, does not condemn ignorance, but obstinacy. This is the necessary result of our definition of faith, and all its branches should spring from the universal rule above given, and from the evident aim and object of the Bible, unless we choose to mix our own inventions therewith. Thus it is not true doctrines which are expressly required by the Bible, so much as doctrines necessary for obedience, and to confirm in our hearts the love of our neighbour, wherein (to adopt the words of John) we are in God, and God in us.

As, then, each man's faith must be judged pious or impious only in respect of its producing obedience or obstinacy, and not in respect of its truth; and as no one will dispute that men's dispositions are exceedingly varied, that all do not acquiesce in the same things, but are ruled some by one opinion some by another, so that what moves one to devotion moves another to laughter and contempt, it follows that there can be no doctrines in the Catholic, or universal, religion, which can give rise to controversy among good men. Such doctrines might be pious to some and impious to others, whereas they should be judged solely by their fruits.

To the universal religion, then, belong only such dogmas as are absolutely required in order to attain obedience to God, and without which such obedience would be impossible; as for the rest, each man—seeing that he is the best judge of his own character should adopt whatever he thinks best adapted to strengthen his love of justice. If this were so, I think there would be no further occasion for controversies in the Church.

I have now no further fear in enumerating the dogmas of universal faith or the fundamental dogmas of the whole of Scripture, inasmuch as they all tend (as may be seen from what has been said) to this one doctrine, namely, that there exists a God, that is, a Supreme Being, Who loves justice and charity, and Who must be obeyed by whosoever would be saved; that the worship of this Being consists in the practice of justice and love towards one's neighbour, and that they contain nothing beyond the following doctrines :-

I. That God or a Supreme Being exists, sovereignly just and merciful, the Exemplar of the true life; that whosoever is ignorant of or disbelieves in His existence cannot obey Him or know Him as a Judge.

II. That He is One. Nobody will dispute that this doctrine is absolutely necessary for entire devotion, admiration, and love towards God. For devotion, admiration, and love spring from the superiority of one over all else.

III. That He is omnipresent, or that all things are open to Him, for if anything could be supposed to be concealed from Him, or to be unnoticed by, Him, we might doubt or be ignorant of the equity of His judgment as directing all things.

IV. That He has supreme right and dominion over all things, and that He does nothing under compulsion, but by His absolute fiat and grace. All things are bound to obey Him, He is not bound to obey any.

V. That the worship of God consists only in justice and charity, or love towards one's neighbour.

VI. That all those, and those only, who obey God by their manner of life are saved; the rest of mankind, who live under the sway of their pleasures, are lost. If we did not believe this, there would be no reason for obeying God rather than pleasure.

vii. Lastly, that God forgives the sins of those who repent. No one is free from sin, so that without this belief all would despair of salvation, and there would be no reason for believing in the mercy of God. He who firmly believes that God, out of the mercy and grace with which He directs all things, forgives the sins of men, and who feels his love of God kindled thereby, he, I say, does really, know Christ according to the Spirit, and Christ is in him.

No one can deny that all these doctrines are before all things necessary, to be believed, in order that every man, without exception, may be able to obey God according to the bidding of the Law above explained, for if one of these precepts be disregarded obedience is destroyed. But as to what God, or the Exemplar of the true life, may be, whether fire, or spirit, or light, or thought, or what not, this, I say, has nothing to do with faith any more than has the question how He comes to be the Exemplar of the true life, whether it be because He has a just and merciful mind, or because all things exist and act through Him, and consequently that we understand through Him, and through Him see what is truly just and good. Everyone may think on such questions as he likes,

Furthermore, faith is not affected, whether we hold that God is omnipresent essentially or potentially; that He directs all things by absolute fiat, or by the necessity of His nature; that He dictates laws like a prince, or that He sets them forth as eternal truths; that man obeys Him by virtue of free will, or by virtue of the necessity of the Divine decree; lastly, that the reward of the good and the punishment of the wicked is natural or supernatural: these and such like questions have no bearing on faith, except in so far as they are used as means to give us license to sin more, or to obey God less. I will go further, and maintain that every man is bound to adapt these dogmas to his own way of thinking, and to interpret them according as he feels that he can give them his fullest and most unhesitating assent, so that he may the more easily obey God with his whole heart.

Such was the manner, as we have already pointed out, in which the faith was in old time revealed and written, in accordance with the understanding and opinions of the prophets and people of the period; so, in like fashion, every man is bound to adapt it to his own opinions, so that he may accept it without any hesitation or mental repugnance. We have shown that faith does not so much re quire truth as piety, and that it is only quickening and pious through obedience, consequently no one is faithful save by obedience alone. The best faith is not necessarily possessed by him who displays the best reasons, but by him who displays the best fruits of justice and charity. How salutary and necessary this doctrine is for a state, in order that men may dwell together in peace and concord; and how many and how great causes of disturbance and crime are thereby cut off, I leave everyone to judge for himself!

Before we go further, I may remark that we can, by means of what we have just proved, easily answer the objections raised in Chap. I., when we were discussing God's speaking with the Israelites on Mount Sinai. For, though the voice heard by the Israelites could not give those men any philosophical or mathematical certitude of God's existence, it was yet sufficient to thrill them with admiration for God, as they already knew Him, and to stir them up to obedience: and such was the object of the display. God did not wish to teach the Israelites the absolute attributes of His essence (none of which He then revealed), but to break down their hardness of heart, and to draw them to obedience: therefore He did not appeal to them with reasons, but with the sound of trumpets, thunder, and lightnings.

It remains for me to show that between faith or theology, and philosophy, there is no connection, nor affinity. I think no one will dispute the fact who has knowledge of the aim and foundations of the two subjects, for they are as wide apart as the poles.

Philosophy has no end in view save truth: faith, as we have abundantly proved, looks for nothing but obedience and piety. Again, philosophy is based on axioms which must be sought from nature alone: faith is based on history and language, and must be sought for only in Scripture and revelation, as we showed in Chap. VII. Faith, therefore, allows the greatest latitude in philosophic speculation, allowing us without blame to think what we like about anything, and only condemning, as heretics and schismatics, those who teach opinions which tend to produce obstinacy, hatred, strife, and anger; while, on the other hand, only considering as faithful those who persuade us, as far as their reason and faculties will permit, to follow justice and charity.

Lastly, as what we are now setting forth are the most important subjects of my treatise, I would most urgently beg the reader, before I proceed, to read these two chapters with especial attention, and to take the trouble to weigh them well in his mind: let him take for granted that I have not written with a view to introducing novelties, but in order to do away with abuses, such as I hope I may, at some future time, at last see reformed.

CHAPTER XV

Theology is Shown Not to be Subservient To Reason, Nor Reason to Theology: A Definition of the Reason Which Enables Us To Accept the Authority of the Bible.

THOSE who know not that philosophy and reason are distinct, dispute whether Scripture should be made subservient to reason, or reason to Scripture: that is, whether the meaning of Scripture should be made to agreed with reason; or whether reason should be made to agree with Scripture: the latter position is assumed by the sceptics who deny the certitude of reason, the former by the dogmatists. Both parties are, as I have shown, utterly in the wrong, for either doctrine would require us to tamper with reason or with Scripture.

We have shown that Scripture does not teach philosophy, but merely obedience, and that all it contains has been adapted to the understanding and established opinions of the multitude. Those, therefore, who wish to adapt it to philosophy, must needs ascribe to the prophets many ideas which they never even dreamed of, and give an extremely forced interpretation to their words: those on the other hand, who would make reason and philosophy subservient to theology, will be forced to accept as Divine utterances the prejudices of the ancient Jews, and to fill and confuse their mind therewith. In short, one party will run wild with the aid of reason, and the other will run wild without the aid of reason.

The first among the Pharisees who openly maintained that Scripture should be made to agree with reason, was Maimonides, whose opinion we reviewed, and abundantly refuted in Chap. VIII.: now, although this writer had much authority among his contemporaries, he was deserted on this question by almost all, and the majority went straight over to the opinion of a certain R. Jehuda Alpakhar, who, in his anxiety to avoid the error of Maimonides, fell into another, which was its exact contrary. He held that reason should be made subservient, and entirely give way to Scripture. He thought that a passage should not be interpreted metaphorically, simply because it was repugnant to reason, but only in the cases when it is inconsistent with Scripture itself—that is, with its clear doctrines. Therefore he laid down the universal rule, that whatsoever Scripture teaches dogmatically, and affirms expressly, must on its own sole authority be admitted as absolutely true: that there is no doctrine in the Bible which directly contradicts the general tenour of the whole: but only some which appear to involve a difference, for the phrases of Scripture often seem to imply something contrary to what has been expressly taught. Such phrases, and such phrases only, we may interpret metaphorically.

For instance, Scripture clearly teaches the unity of God (see Deut. vi:4), nor is there any text distinctly asserting a plurality of gods; but in several passages God speaks of Himself, and the prophets speak of Him, in the plural number; such phrases are simply a manner of speaking, and do not mean that there actually are several gods: they are to be explained metaphorically, not because a plurality of gods is repugnant to reason, but because Scripture distinctly asserts that there is only one.

So, again, as Scripture asserts (as Alpakhar thinks) in Deut. iv:15, that God is incorporeal, we are bound, solely by the authority of this text, and not by reason, to believe that God has no body: consequently we must explain metaphorically, on the sole authority of Scripture, all those passages which attribute to God hands, feet, &c., and take them merely as figures of speech. Such is the opinion of Alpakhar. In so far as he seeks to explain Scripture by Scripture, I praise him, but I marvel that a man gifted with reason should wish to debase that faculty. It is true that Scripture should be explained by Scripture, so long as we are in difficulties about the meaning and intention of the prophets, but when we have elicited the true meaning, we must of necessity make use of our judgment and reason in order to assent thereto. If reason, however, much as she rebels, is to be entirely subjected to Scripture, I ask, are we to effect her submission by her own aid, or without her, and blindly? If the latter, we shall surely act foolishly and injudiciously; if the former, we assent to Scripture under the dominion of reason, and should not assent to it without her. Moreover, I may ask now, is a man to assent to anything against his reason? What is denial if it be not reason's refusal to assent? In short, I am astonished that anyone should wish to subject reason, the greatest of gifts and a light from on high, to the dead letter which may have been corrupted by human malice; that it should be thought no crime to speak with contempt of mind, the true handwriting of God's Word, calling it corrupt, blind, and lost, while it is considered the greatest of crimes to say the same of the letter, which is merely the reflection and image of God's Word. Men think it pious to trust nothing to reason and their own judgment, and impious to doubt the faith of those who have transmitted to us the sacred books. Such conduct is not piety, but mere folly. And, after all, why are they so anxious? What are they afraid of? Do they think that faith and religion cannot be upheld unless—men purposely keep themselves in ignorance, and turn their backs on reason? If this be so, they have but a timid trust in Scripture.

However, be it far from me to say that religion should seek to enslave reason, or reason religion, or that both should not be able to keep their sovereignty in perfect harmony. I will revert to this question presently, for I wish now to discuss Alpakhar's rule.

He requires, as we have stated, that we should accept as true, or reject as false, everything asserted or denied by Scripture, and he further states that Scripture never expressly asserts or denies anything which contradicts its assertions or negations elsewhere. The rashness of such a requirement and statement can escape no one. For (passing over the fact that he does not notice that Scripture consists of different books, written at different times, for different people, by different authors:

45

and also that his requirement is made on his own authority without any corroboration from reason or Scripture) he would be bound to show that all passages which are indirectly contradictory of the rest, can be satisfactorily explained metaphorically through the nature of the language and the context: further, that Scripture has come down to us untampered with. However, we will go into the matter at length.

Firstly, I ask what shall we do if reason prove recalcitrant? Shall we still be bound to affirm whatever Scripture affirms, and to deny whatever Scripture denies? Perhaps it will be answered that Scripture contains nothing repugnant to reason. But I insist !hat it expressly affirms and teaches that God is jealous (namely, in the decalogue itself, and in Exod. xxxiv:14, and in Deut. iv:24, and in many other places), and I assert that such a doctrine is repugnant to reason. It must, I suppose, in spite of all, be accepted as true. If there are any passages in Scripture which imply that God is not jealous, they must be taken metaphorically as meaning nothing of the kind. So, also, Scripture expressly states (Exod. xix:20, &c.) that God came down to Mount Sinai, and it attributes to Him other movements from place to place, nowhere directly stating that God does not so move. Wherefore, we must take the passage literally, and Solomon's words (I Kings viii:27), "But will God dwell on the earth? Behold the heavens and earth cannot contain thee," inasmuch as they do not expressly state that God does not move from place to place, but only imply it, must be explained away till they have no further semblance of denying locomotion to the Deity. So also we must believe that the sky is the habitation and throne of God, for Scripture expressly says so; and similarly many passages expressing the opinions of the prophets or the multitude, which reason and philosophy, but not Scripture, tell us to be false, must be taken as true if we are io follow the guidance of our author, for according to him, reason has nothing to do with the matter. Further, it is untrue that Scripture never contradicts itself directly, but only by implication. For Moses says, in so many words (Deut. iv:24), "The Lord thy God is a consuming fire," and elsewhere expressly denies that God has any

A THEOLOGICO-POLITICAL TREATISE (PART III)

likeness to visible things. (Deut. iv. 12.) If it be decided that the latter passage only contradicts the former by implication, and must be adapted thereto, lest it seem to negative it, let us grant that God is a fire; or rather, lest we should seem to have taken leave of our senses, let us pass the matter over and take another example.

Samuel expressly denies that God ever repents, "for he is not a man that he should repent" (I Sam. xv:29). Jeremiah, on the other hand, asserts that God does repent, both of the evil and of the good which He had intended to do (Jer. xviii:8-10). What? Are not these two texts directly contradictory? Which of the two, then, would our author want to explain metaphorically? Both statements are general, and each is the opposite of the other—what one flatly affirms, the other flatly, denies. So, by his own rule, he would be obliged at once to reject them as false, and to accept them as true.

Again, what is the point of one passage, not being contradicted by another directly, but only by implication, if the implication is clear, and the nature and context of the passage preclude metaphorical interpretation? There are many such instances in the Bible, as we saw in Chap. ii. (where we pointed out that the prophets held different and contradictory opinions), and also in Chaps. ix. and x., where we drew attention to the contradictions in the historical narratives. There is no need for me to go through them all again, for what I have said sufficiently exposes the absurdities which would follow from an opinion and rule such as we are discussing, and shows the hastiness of its propounder.

We may, therefore, put this theory, as well as that of Maimonides, entirely out of court; and we may, take it for indisputable that theology is not bound to serve reason, nor reason theology, but that each has her own domain.

The sphere of reason is, as we have said, truth and wisdom; the sphere of theology, is piety and obedience. The power of reason does not extend so far as to determine for us that men may be blessed through simple obedience, without understanding.

Theology, tells us nothing else, enjoins on us no command save obedience, and has neither the will nor the power to oppose reason: she defines the dogmas of faith (as we pointed out in the last chapter) only in so far as they may be necessary, for obedience, and leaves reason to determine their precise truth: for reason is the light of the mind, and without her all things are dreams and phantoms.

By theology, I here mean, strictly speaking, revelation, in so far as it indicates the object aimed at by Scripture namely, the scheme and manner of obedience, or the true dogmas of piety and faith. This may truly be called the Word of God, which does not consist in a certain number of books (see Chap. xii.). Theology thus understood, if we regard its precepts or rules of life, will be found in accordance with reason; and, if we look to its aim and object, will be seen to be in nowise repugnant thereto, wherefore it is universal to all men.

As for its bearing on Scripture, we have shown in Chap. vii. that the meaning of Scripture should be gathered from its own history, and not from the history of nature in general, which is the basis of philosophy.

We ought not to be hindered if we find that our investigation of the meaning of Scripture thus conducted shows us that it is here and there repugnant to reason; for whatever we may find of this sort in the Bible, which men may be in ignorance of, without injury to their charity, has, we may be sure, no bearing on theology or the Word of God, and may, therefore, without blame, be viewed by every one as he pleases.

To sum up, we may draw the absolute conclusion that the Bible must not be accommodated to reason, nor reason to the Bible.

Now, inasmuch as the basis of theology—the doctrine that man may be saved by obedience alone—cannot be proved by reason whether it be true or false, we may be asked, Why, then, should we believe it? If we do so without the aid of reason, we accept it blindly, and act foolishly and injudiciously; if, on the other hand, we settle that it can be proved by reason, theology becomes a part of philosophy, and inseparable therefrom.

But I make answer that I have absolutely established that this basis of theology cannot be investigated by the natural light of reason, or, at any rate, that no one ever has proved it by such means, and, therefore, revelation was necessary. We should, however, make use of our reason, in order to grasp with moral certainty what is revealed—I say, with moral certainty, for we cannot hope to attain greater certainty, than the prophets: yet their certainty was only, moral, as I showed in Chap. II.

Those, therefore, who attempt to set forth the authority of Scripture with mathematical demonstrations are wholly in error: for the authority, of the Bible is dependent on the authority of the prophets, and can be supported by no stronger arguments than those employed in old time by the prophets for convincing the people of their own authority. Our certainty on the same subject can be founded on no other basis than that which served as foundation for the certainty of the prophets.

Now the certainty of the prophets consisted (as we pointed out) in these elements:

I. A distinct and vivid imagination.

II. A sign.

III. Lastly, and chiefly, a mind turned to what is just and good. It was based on no other reasons than these, and consequently they cannot prove their authority by any other reasons, either to the multitude whom they addressed orally, nor to us whom they address in writing.

The first of these reasons, namely, the vivid imagination, could be valid only for the prophets; therefore, our certainty concerning revelation must, and ought to be, based on the remaining two—namely, the sign and the teaching. Such is the express doctrine of Moses, for (in Deut. xviii.) he bids the people obey the prophet who should give a true sign in the name of the Lord, but if he should predict falsely, even though it were in the name of the Lord, he should be put to death, as should also he who strives to lead away the people from the true religion, though he confirm his authority with signs and portents. We may compare with the above Deut. xiii. Whence it follows that a true prophet could be distinguished from a false one, both by his doctrine and by the miracles he wrought, for Moses declares such an one to be a true prophet, and bids the people trust him without fear of deceit. He condemns as false, and worthy, of death, those who predict anything falsely even in the name of the Lord, or who preach false gods, even though their miracles be real.

The only reason, then, which we have for belief in Scripture or the writings of the prophets, is the doctrine we find therein, and the signs by which it is confirmed. For as we see that the prophets extol charity and justice above all things, and have no other object, we conclude that they did not write from unworthy motives, but because they really thought that men might become blessed through obedience and faith: further, as we see that they confirmed their teaching with signs and wonders, we become persuaded that they did not speak at random, nor run riot in their prophecies. We are further strengthened in our conclusion by the fact that the morality they teach is in evident agreement with reason, for it is no accidental coincidence that the Word of God which we find in the prophets coincides with the Word of God written in our hearts. We may, I say, conclude this from the sacred books as certainly as did the Jews of old from the living voice of the prophets: for we showed in Chap. xii. that Scripture has come down to us intact in respect to its doctrine and main narratives.

Therefore this whole basis of theology and Scripture, though it does not admit of mathematical proof, may yet be accepted with the approval of our judgment. It would be folly to refuse to accept what is confirmed by such ample prophetic testimony, and what has proved such a comfort to those whose reason is comparatively weak, and such a benefit to the state; a doctrine, moreover, which we may believe in without the slightest peril or hurt, and should reject simply because it cannot be mathematically proved: it is as though we should admit nothing as true, or as a wise rule of life, which could ever, in any possible way, be called in question; or as though most of our actions were not full of uncertainty and hazards.

I admit that those who believe that theology and philosophy are mutually contradictory, and that therefore either one or the other must be thrust from its throne—I admit, I say, that such persons are not unreasonable in attempting to put theology on a firm basis, and to demonstrate its truth mathematically. Who, unless he were desperate or mad, would wish to bid an incontinent farewell to reason, or to despise the arts and sciences, or to deny reason's certitude? But, in the meanwhile, we cannot wholly absolve them from blame, inasmuch as they invoke the aid of reason for her own defeat, and attempt infallibly to prove her fallible. While they are trying to prove mathematically the authority and truth of theology, and to take away the authority of natural reason, they are in reality only bringing theology under reason's dominion, and proving that her authority has no weight unless natural reason be at the back of it.

If they boast that they themselves assent because of the inward testimony of the Holy Spirit, and that they only invoke the aid of reason because of unbelievers, in order to convince them, not even so can this meet with our approval, for we can easily show that they have spoken either from emotion or vain-glory. It most clearly follows from the last chapter that the Holy Spirit only gives its testimony in favour of works, called by Paul (in Gal. v:22) the fruits of the Spirit, and is in itself really nothing but the mental acquiescence which follows a good action in our souls. No spirit gives testimony concerning the certitude of matters within the sphere of speculation, save only reason, who is mistress, as we have shown, of the whole realm of truth. If then they assert that they possess this Spirit which makes them certain of truth, they speak falsely, and according to the prejudices of the emotions, or else they are in great dread lest they should be vanquished by philosophers and exposed to public ridicule, and therefore they flee, as it were, to the altar; but their refuge is vain, for what altar will shelter a man who has outraged reason? However, I pass such persons over, for I think I have fulfilled my purpose, and shown how philosophy should be separated from theology, and wherein each consists; that neither should be subservient to the other, but that each should keep her unopposed dominion. Lastly, as occasion offered, I have pointed out the absurdities, the inconveniences, and the evils following from the extraordinary confusion which has hitherto prevailed between the two subjects, owing to their not being properly distinguished and separated. Before I go further I would expressly state (though I have said it before) that I consider the utility and the need for Holy Scripture or Revelation to be very great. For as we cannot perceive by the natural light of reason that simple obedience is the path of salvation,[2] and are taught by revelation only that it is so by the special grace of God, which our reason cannot attain, it follows that the Bible has brought a very great consolation to mankind. All are able to obey, whereas there are but very few, compared with the aggregate of humanity, who can acquire the habit of virtue under the unaided guidance of reason. Thus if we had not the testimony of Scripture, we should doubt of the salvation of nearly all men.

END OF PART III

---

2   See Endnote 25.

Author's Endnotes to the

Theologico-Political Treatise

CHAPTERS XI TO XV

CHAPTER XI.

Endnote 24. "Now I think." The translators render the {Greek} word "I infer", and assert that Paul uses it as synonymous with {a Greek word}. But the former word has, in Greek, the same meaning as the Hebrew word rendered to think, to esteem, to judge. And this signification would be in entire agreement with the Syriac translation. This Syriac translation (if it be a translation, which is very doubtful, for we know neither the time of its appearance, nor the translators and Syriac was the vernacular of the Apostles) renders the text before us in a way well explained by Tremellius as "we think, therefore."

CHAPTER XV.

Endnote 25. "That simple obedience is the path of salvation." In other words, it is enough for salvation or blessedness, that we should embrace the Divine decrees as laws or commands; there is no need to conceive them as eternal truths. This can be taught us by Revelation, not Reason, as appears from the demonstrations given in Chapter iv.

End of Endnotes to PART III.